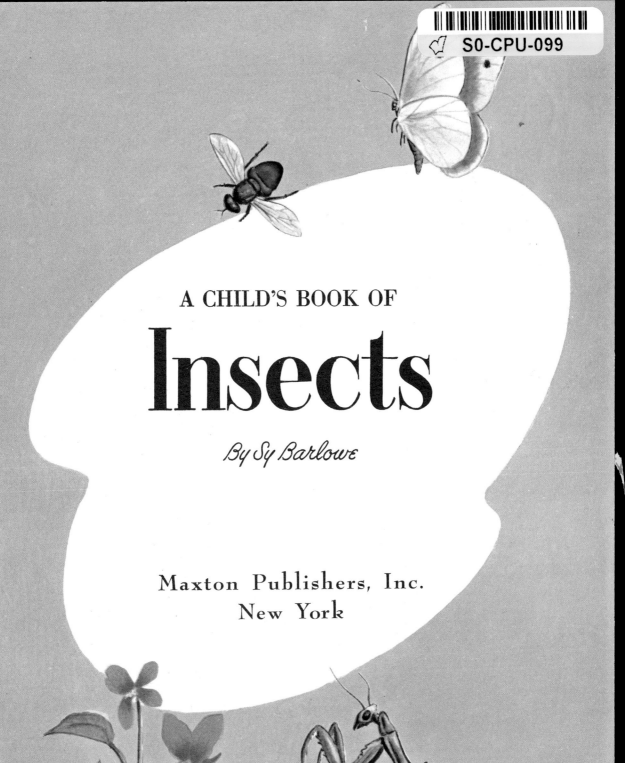

A CHILD'S BOOK OF
Insects

By Sy Barlowe

Maxton Publishers, Inc.
New York

─────TRUE SIZE OF INSECTS─────

Because some of the insects illustrated in this book are very small, these are shown greatly enlarged so that you may be able to identify them more easily. In those instances you will find at the end of the description a small outline drawing which shows the true size of the insect.

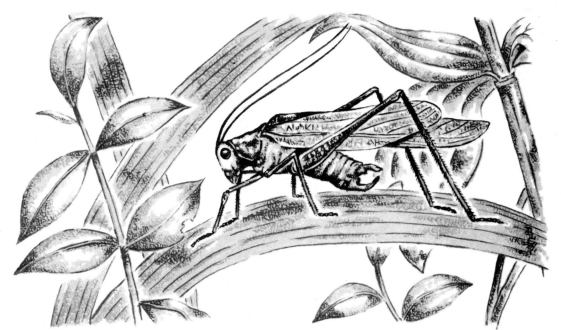

Katydid

Have you ever wondered what it was that made the familiar sound, "Katy did, Katy she did, she did," on a summer night or on a cloudy day? If you look closely in the daytime, you might find this little green grasshopper. Its coloring, which is so much like the leaves it sits on, helps to hide it from its enemies. This is called protective coloration.

Some Katydids live in trees and feed on the leaves while others seem to prefer to spend their time in the grass, tall weeds, or bushes during the day.

The song we spoke of before is made by Mr. Katydid rubbing the bases of his wing covers together, much like a person playing on a fiddle.

Eggs are laid in the fall and the young are born the fol-

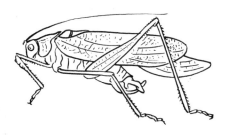

lowing spring. They look very much like their parents but lack wings, which develop later as they grow. There is no pupal stage.

American Locust

A champion long-distance jumper is the familiar Locust of our fields and meadows. It is quite often considered a serious pest as it will eat almost any kind of plant, and that doesn't make it too popular with Farmer Jones.

Mrs. Locust lays her eggs underground in the spring and they hatch into what are called "nymphs." These "nymphs," or baby Locusts, look like their mothers but do not have wings. They shed their skins about 5 times before they become full-grown adults.

When the area in which the Locusts are living cannot accommodate their increasing population, they swarm in countless numbers and fly to other places eating large amounts of plants and crops on their destructive way.

Praying Mantis

egg case

A welcome guest in our gardens is the Praying Mantis, for it destroys many harmful pests.

Although it can fly, it prefers to wait on a tree or shrub until an unsuspecting insect comes by. As soon as the Mantis sees its intended dinner, it moves quietly and carefully toward it. Then suddenly, like a flash of lightning, the forelegs shoot out and the victim is caught.

The female lays small groups of eggs that are surrounded by a protective covering. These are attached to a board, twigs, or even a building. They hatch in May or June into tiny Mantes that look just like their parents, lacking only the wings. A male Mantis is liable to be eaten by his mate if he is not careful.

A Mantis kept in a glass tank makes an interesting pet, if you are willing to supply it with live insects.

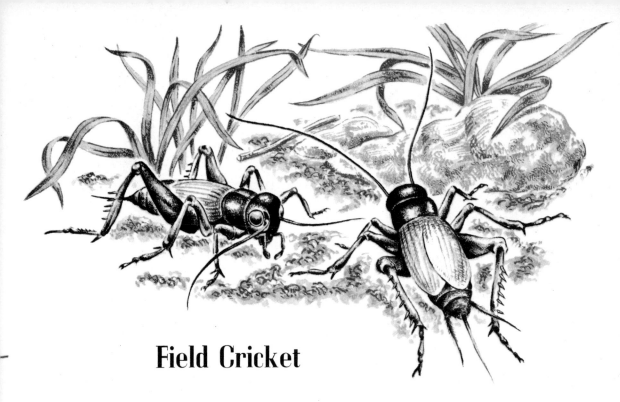

Field Cricket

Who hasn't heard the merry chirping of a Cricket on a warm summer night? This familiar evening concert is really the love song of the male Cricket, and is accomplished by rubbing the fore wings together.

The brown or black Field Crickets are to be found everywhere in gardens, pastures, under stones, and even sometimes in dwellings. When they invade our homes, they may injure and destroy food, clothing, and the like. They are quite injurious to crops and vegetation and do most of their harmful work at night, when they are least likely to be disturbed. Though they prefer a vegetable diet, they may attack and eat other insects and also each other.

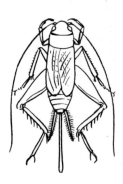

The female lays several hundred eggs in holes in the ground. The baby Cricket looks just like its parents, except it doesn't have developed wings.

You may be surprised to learn that Crickets' ears are located on their front legs.

Dobson-fly

A very fierce-looking fellow is the male Dobson-fly with his long crossed jaws and a 4 to 5 inch wing-spread, but you needn't worry, he is quite harmless.

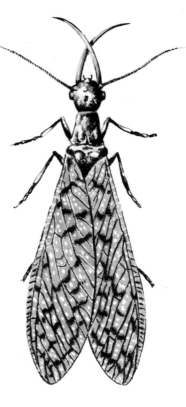

The female lays a mass of several thousand eggs on plants, stones, or other objects overhanging the water. The eggs hatch into larvae that drop into the water.

These "nymphs," or larvae, are the familiar hellgrammites that are well known to fishermen as one of the best baits for bass, trout, and perch. They live beneath stones in the shallow rapids of streams and rivers, feeding on all sorts of water insects. They can swim but usually crawl.

After about 35 months the larvae leave the water and spend a month as a pupa. They then emerge and become adult winged Dobson-flies.

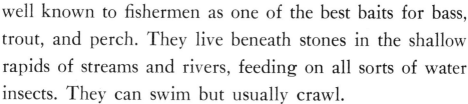

larva
hellgrammite

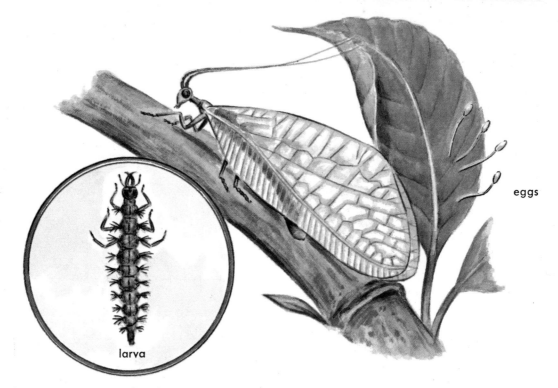

eggs

larva

Green Lacewing

The delicate green Lacewing, sometimes known as Golden-eye, is to be found on plants in our orchards and gardens. Often called "Greenflies," although not true flies, both the adult Lacewings and larvae will eat large quantities of aphids. Because the larvae feed on aphids so heartily they are called aphid-lions. Aphids are small, harmful plant insects.

The mother Lacewing has a most interesting manner of laying her eggs. The tip of her abdomen touches a leaf or twig and releases a small amount of fluid. Then she lifts her abdomen and the fluid is drawn out like a thread and an egg is laid on the end.

This method of laying eggs is used for a good reason. When they hatch, the larvae are so hungry that the first  one out would eat up all the rest if they weren't protected by stalks of their own.

Ant Lion

It is hard to imagine that the harmless, slender, gauzy-winged adult Ant Lion is in any way connected with its fierce larvae.

The female lays her eggs on the ground. When they hatch, the larva burrows into the sandy soil, making a pitfall to trap any unwary ants that may fall in. When an ant, or other wingless creature, comes up to the edge of the pit, the sand crumbles under its feet and it tumbles into the powerful jaws of the waiting Ant Lion larva lying buried at the bottom. Once its prey is in its grasp, the Ant Lion's jaws never let go for a moment until the victim is sucked dry of body juices.

The jaws of the larva are hollow, and made for sucking as well as grasping.

It may take from 1 to 3 years for the larva to mature. As it grows it builds a globular silken cocoon about the size of a large pea in which it pupates.

Ant Lion larva in pit

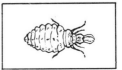

Giant Water Bug

This very large bug, 2 to 4 inches long, is also known as the Electric Light Bug, because it is attracted by strong lights and sometimes gathers in large numbers around them.

The powerful forelegs are used to capture other water insects, frogs, and small fish. These bugs have been known to kill fish four times their own size, and may invade fish hatcheries, where they destroy eggs, young, and even the adult fish.

Eggs of the Giant Water Bug hatch in 1 to 2 weeks, the young being little copies of the parents, with the exception of the wing development. They go through 5 stages of growth before they mature.

The Smaller Giant Water Bug, a close relative, resembles the one pictured in everything but size. The female of this species fastens the fertilized eggs to the back of the male, where he carries them until they hatch.

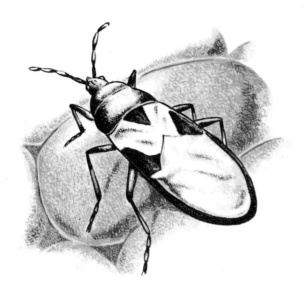

Chinch Bug

This villain is considered one of the six worst insect pests in America, and the unhappy farmer wishes it had stayed in its original home in the tropics. It makes up in numbers what it lacks in size, for it is a small fellow.

After spending the winter in corn shacks and grass tufts, Chinch Bugs fly to grain fields. Here the female lays about 500 eggs in the roots or at the base of the plants. These eggs hatch in about 2 weeks into little yellow "nymphs" that begin their destructive lives by sucking the juices of the plants, causing them to wilt and die. They spend about 40 days as "nymphs," laying waste large areas of corn fields (their favorite food) and other grain fields.

The damage caused by these pests has been known to run into millions of dollars every year. The short time spent in the nymph stage allows the Chinch Bug to develop as many as 2 or 3 generations in a single season.

Chinch Bugs seem to have found ideal living conditions in the Mississippi Valley, where they are more destructive and abundant than anywhere else.

nymph

Harlequin Stinkbug

Don't let its gay coat fool you, for the Harlequin Stinkbug is no clown or laughing matter. Considered by many to be one of our worst pests, it does, however, have its interesting side. Its eggs, which number an even dozen, are neatly arranged, and look very much like tiny white decorated beer barrels, 6 in a row.

It is believed that the disagreeable odor that this and other members of the Stinkbug family give off is a means of discouraging birds and other enemies from eating them.

Our farmers in the South have a special dislike for this insect, for that is where it does the most damage. It can be found hard at work destroying such crops as cabbages, turnips, and radishes, among many others. It is so fond of cabbage that it is often called the Harlequin Cabbage Bug.

Dragon Fly

The swift-darting Dragon Fly has been falsely thought of as harmful to man, when it really is one of man's best friends in the insect world. Its food consists of the larvae of other water insects and it may eat tadpoles, but its favorites are mosquitoes and flies, and everyone knows how harmful these two can be.

We can tell the difference between the Dragon Fly and the smaller Damsel Fly, which looks very much like it, by the positions of the wings when they are at rest. The Dragon Fly holds its wings outspread, while the Damsel Fly folds its wings over its back.

Mrs. Dragon Fly places her eggs in the mud or water. In several weeks they hatch, and out come the nymphs who spend their time wandering about the bottom of a muddy pond feeding on water bugs, caddis worms, and the like.

nymph

Caddis Fly

Soft bodies and a general mothlike appearance identify the adult Caddis Fly. Its wings are usually held sloping over the back like a slanting roof. Caddis Flies are shy creatures and are seldom seen except when they gather around bright lights to which they are attracted in large numbers.

The young of the Caddis Fly, the Caddis Worm or larva, are more interesting than the adults. These clever little creatures build long tubes of various materials in which they live in comparative safety.

The different species of Caddis Worms each use a particular type of material to build their houses, like small sticks and straw, shells, and stones. When the Caddis Worm is ready to change into a pupa, it seals both ends of its home with silk, spends the

necessary time within, and then emerges as a full-grown Caddis Fly.

Caddis worm

Firefly

This is not really a fly at all, but a soft-bodied beetle. These wonderful little creatures shine like fairy lamps in the soft darkness of a summer night. There are as many as fifty different kinds of Fireflies in the United States but not all of them emit light.

larva

The amazing way in which these insects are able to produce light without any waste of energy in heat has challenged scientists for many years. The light is produced in the abdomen and is not continuous, but flashes on and off, thus enabling the Fireflies to find their mates.

Wingless females and the larvae are called Glow Worms, and it is interesting to note that the eggs and larvae of some species will also glow. The larvae live in rubbish, rotted wood, or in the soil, feeding on other insects.

In tropical regions, a most wonderful sight is said to be the flashing, every 10 seconds, of thousands of Fireflies all at the same time.

Tiger Beetle

This brightly colored, metallic green beetle with its long thin legs is probably not too often seen at close range because it is rather difficult to capture.

larva

Tiger Beetles are to be found on the shores of streams, woodland trails, and on hot days on dusty roads. At night, they retire to holes in the ground or under stones.

The eggs are laid singly in the soil, and the larvae are just as fierce but not so pretty as their parents. They are sometimes known as "Doodlebugs." They dig deep burrows, then wait at the top to catch any careless insect that might pass by. They are even equipped with hooks on their backs which prevent them from being pulled out of their burrows by a stronger insect. The larvae will seal off the entrance hole and pupate in the burrow.

Japanese Beetle

A very undesirable immigrant, this shiny green Beetle was accidentally introduced into this country in 1916 from Japan and is quite a serious pest now. Some natural enemies of this insect have been imported from Japan in an effort to control the Japanese Beetle.

The food of this beetle and its larvae is many kinds of cultivated trees and shrubs, such as grapes, strawberries, blackberries, apples, cherries, and corn, as well as roses and other valuable plants.

Tiny white eggs are laid in the ground sometime in the month of July. The larvae, which are white, hatch from these eggs, and spend the summer feeding. They hibernate during the winter, enter the pupal stage during the spring, and emerge as adults in June or July.

Ladybird Beetle

This is among the most useful of all insects and should be treated like the good friend of man that it is. Ladybird Beetles are usually red, black, or yellow, and spotted with white, red, yellow, or black.

pupa

They feed on aphids (plant lice) and the eggs of some very harmful insects, such as the Chinch Bug, Colorado Potato Beetle, and many others. When an Australian insect pest was ruining the fruit trees in California, an Australian Ladybird Beetle was imported and in a short time the pest was completely wiped out.

Eggs are laid in the spring. The larvae eat insect eggs and small insects. The mature larvae then becomes a pupa, and hangs head down for a few days before becoming an adult.

larva

Colorado Potato Beetle

At one time this insect was quietly confining its feeding to unimportant plants in the Rocky Mountain area. It was in the year 1850, when the settlers began to grow potatoes, that this member of the Leaf Beetle family developed a brand-new taste. By 1874 it had spread eastward and had reached the Atlantic Coast, and now can be found wherever potatoes are grown except in California. It has even reached Europe.

larva

The yellow eggs are laid on the underside of potato leaves. These hatch in about a week and the larvae which are fat, soft, and white, feed on the leaves. The larvae burrow underground, change into pupae, and then in about 2 weeks come out as adults that continue to feed on the potato plants.

Black Swallowtail Butterfly

This is the largest of our butterflies, with a wingspread up to 4 inches. It is found throughout the United States.

The Black Swallowtail is a day flier, as are all butterflies.

The eggs are yellow-brown, smooth, round, laid singly on the underside of leaves, and hatch in 5 to 10 days. The larva is large and smooth-skinned. It feeds on the leaves of carrots, parsnips, caraway, and other similar plants. It is capable of producing a strong, disagreeable odor when disturbed, which is a protection. After attaching itself to a twig or branch, it pupates for 9 days in an upright position, with the chrysalis resting on its tail.

caterpillar

chrysalis

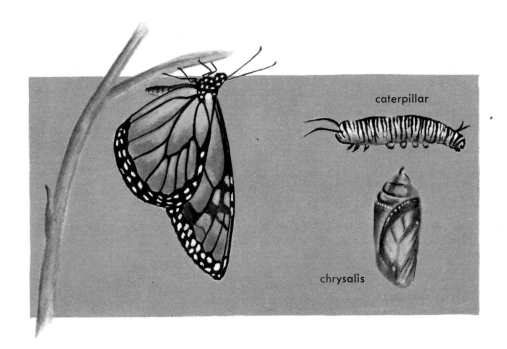

caterpillar

chrysalis

Monarch Butterfly

Monarch Butterflies, also known as Milkweed Butterflies, are to be found in fields and on roadsides. In the fall they migrate in large groups to the extreme south of the United States and even farther, to the West Indies and Central and South America.

The pale green eggs are laid on milkweed leaves and hatch in about 4 days. The larva (caterpillar) feeds on the milkweed leaves, sheds its skin 4 times in about 10 days, then attaches itself to a leaf, pupates in a pale green chrysalis spotted with gold and black for about 12 days. Then the wonderful miracle of the insect world—we see a beautiful adult Monarch Butterfly emerge from the chrysalis.

The Monarch Butterfly bears the distinction of being imitated to a startling degree by the Viceroy Butterfly, who is no relation. The Monarch seems to be quite distasteful to its bird enemies, which explains why the Viceroy mimics it.

Cabbage Butterfly

Another unwelcome guest who is not native to our land, but who came from Europe in 1860 and is now well established here, is the Cabbage Butterfly. This butterfly and its larvae 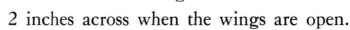 are more injurious to the agricultural industry in this country than any other species of butterfly.

The Cabbage Butterfly is white with black dots on each forewing and measures about 2 inches across when the wings are open. It is especially fond of cabbage and cauliflower but does not confine itself to those plants.

caterpillar

chrysalis

The eggs of this butterfly are yellow, laid singly on the undersides of leaves, and hatch in about 1 week. The larvae are green and become full grown in about 2 weeks. Then the green chrysalis is formed which lasts for about 10 days.

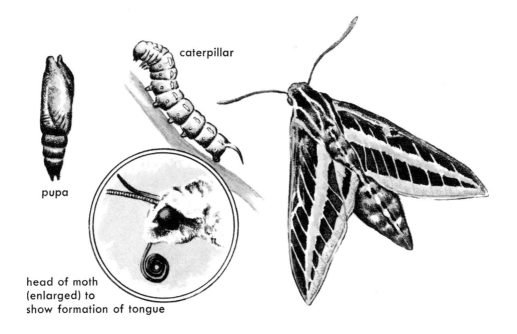

caterpillar

pupa

head of moth
(enlarged) to
show formation of tongue

White-Lined Sphinx Moth

There are about one hundred species of Sphinx Moths in this country. They are very often mistaken for humming-birds because of their large size (5-inch wingspread) and their habit of hovering over flowers with wings beating so rapidly as to be invisible.

This moth is equipped with a marvelous tongue, which is really a sucking tube, and when not in use is coiled up underneath the head like a watch spring. This long tongue enables the moth to obtain nectar and pollinate such flowers as petunias, honeysuckle, and other tubular flowers.

The larvae, which hatch from large, shiny green eggs, are green, have a horn on the tail, and are therefore some-times known as Hornworms.

The larvae spend 4 weeks as cater-pillars, then pupate in the soil or among rubbish and leaves on the ground.

Sphinx with wings spread

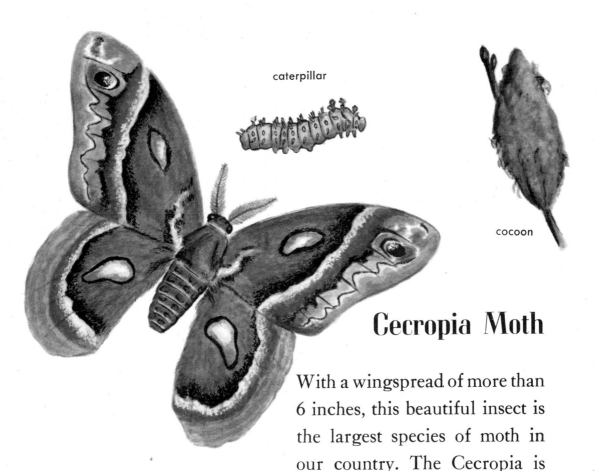

caterpillar

cocoon

Cecropia Moth

With a wingspread of more than 6 inches, this beautiful insect is the largest species of moth in our country. The Cecropia is nocturnal in habit and the adult does not require any food.

Up to 400 pinkish-white eggs are laid in rows on leaves and hatch in about 2 weeks. The larva, which is black, then red, sheds its skin several times, and when mature is green with large yellow, red, and blue tubercles.

The larva feeds on leaves of apple, maple, elm, wild cherry, willow, and many other trees and shrubs.

It then spins a cocoon which is fastened to twigs from which the adult moth emerges in late spring or summer. Some birds with beaks that are strong enough to penetrate the tough cocoons will feed upon the tasty pupa inside the cocoon.

This moth is also known by the name of Emperor Moth.

Luna Moth

Also known as the "Pale Empress of the Night," this beautiful moth is a favorite of amateur collectors.

The Luna as well as the Cecropia is a member of the Giant Silkworm family, whose bodies are comparatively heavy and covered with hair and whose wings are wide and strong.

The white eggs, as many as 200, are fastened to twigs and upper leaf surfaces, hatch in about 3 weeks, and come out clear green caterpillars. After shedding 4 times, and about a month from the time it hatched, the larva or caterpillar spins a thin, leaf-covered cocoon in which the pupa will spend the winter.

Food of the Luna Moth larva consists of the leaves of the walnut, hickory, sweet gum, and many other trees.

actual size

caterpillar

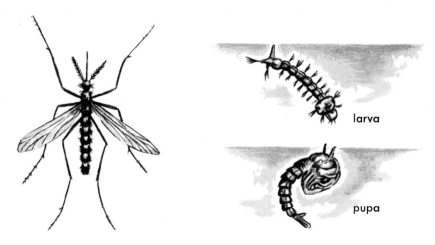

larva

pupa

Mosquitoes

Mosquitoes are known for their disease-carrying abilities. In tropic areas the Malaria Mosquito is responsible for spreading Malaria.

The female of the species is the dangerous one. The male is harmless and is content to satisfy his hunger with nectar and other plant juices.

The eggs of the mosquito are laid in rafts of several hundred, in ponds, ditches, barrels, tin cans, etc. These egg rafts usually hatch in from 1 to 5 days into larvae called "wrigglers." They feed on very small animal life in the water. In a week or two they become pupae and in 4 or 5 days adult mosquitoes.

The mosquito has many natural enemies and forms an important part of the diet of dragonflies, damsel flies, and birds such as flycatchers, swallows, swifts, and night hawks.

malaria mosquito

house mosquito

Flies

fruit fly — ⅛"

Flies are different from most insects, since they seem to be able to fly as well with a single pair of wings as other insects can with two pairs.

Some flies are scavengers and others are effective controls on some harmful insects.

Fruit flies have become important in the laboratories of our scientists in the study of heredity. These little flies are yellowish and about ⅛ of an inch long with bright red eyes.

Like the Mosquito, the female is the villain in the Horse Fly family and few if any animals can outrace this swift-flying pest.

The fisherman or camper is familiar with the pesky Deer Fly that buzzes around his head and also around the ears of horses.

The Robber Fly never attacks man or animal and may be seen preying upon other flies, butterflies, beetles, and moths.

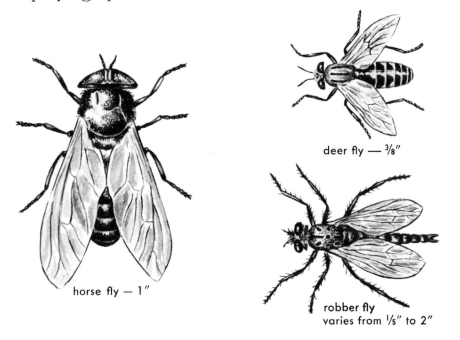

horse fly — 1"

deer fly — ⅜"

robber fly
varies from ⅕" to 2"

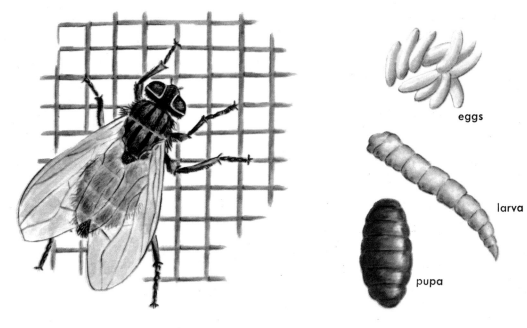

eggs

larva

pupa

House Fly

This is the true villain of the insect world and should be swatted or avoided, whichever is more effective at the moment. Flies are said to be capable of spreading 30 to 40 different diseases. The germs are carried on the hairs of the legs or are swallowed and vomited out again.

Up to 600 eggs are laid in clusters, usually in manure exposed to sunshine. These hatch in a very short time—in warm weather in about 10 hours, or 3 days in cool weather. Larvae are called maggots. These become fully developed in about 5 days; then they pupate for about 5 more days and emerge as full-grown adults.

The time from the egg to the adult fly is about 2 weeks. There are about a dozen generations a year, so you can see that it is possible for one female in April to have 5½ trillion descendants by September.

Cornfield Ant

The life of ants has long been a source of interest to all and makes them favorite objects for study.

The Cornfield Ant is the most common and abundant of all our ants, and is found in fields and on lawns. The ant colony is usually established by a queen, who sheds her wings.

She lays about 200 eggs which produce workers, soldiers, males, and other queens. Once mated, the queen can produce eggs for the rest of her life, which may be as long as 10 or 15 years.

Ants keep aphids (small plant lice) for the honeydew they produce, much the same as we keep cattle. Slave ants are also used to lessen the labor of ants. These ants are seized while they are still larvae and brought home to the nests, to become servants in the colonies of the raiders.

Paper Wasp

The Paper Wasp has red and yellow markings. Paper Wasps produce paper from wood that they chew up, and then use to build their nests. These nests are somewhat unprotected and usually built in some sheltered spot with the cells opening downward.

Only the queen lives through the winter, and she will lay eggs in the nest she has built, feeding the larvae insects, caterpillars, and nectar. This she does until they have developed to the point where they take over the duties of enlarging the nest and obtaining food for the new generations of young that are produced through the summer.

Paper Wasps will not sting unless they are annoyed, and though the sting is painful, it is not dangerous.

It is interesting to note that the mature larva does not pupate in a cocoon but is sealed up in its cell and pupates there.

Paper Wasps are closely related to the other social insects, the hornets and yellowjackets.

Bumblebee

This familiar black-and-golden yellow bee is found in fields of clover or around large fragrant flowers. It is the only bee with a long tongue capable of fertilizing certain red clovers. It is therefore impossible to raise red clover where there are no Bumblebees.

Like the wasp, the queen bee is the only member of the colony that lives through the winter. She starts a new colony in the spring by laying from 400 to 1,000 eggs in wax cells or "combs" that hatch in 4 or 5 days. The larva matures in about 7 days and pupates for about 10 days in the larval cell.

Bumblebees have "pollen baskets" formed by stiff hairs on their hind legs, which are used to carry the pollen back to the underground nests.

Bumblebees also produce honey. Their nests are often dug up and the contents eaten by bears, mice, and other animals.

HOW INSECTS GROW

When insects grow, many times they go through different stages during which they hardly look at all like what they will grow up to be. This series of changes is known as "metamorphosis," which means "change in form."

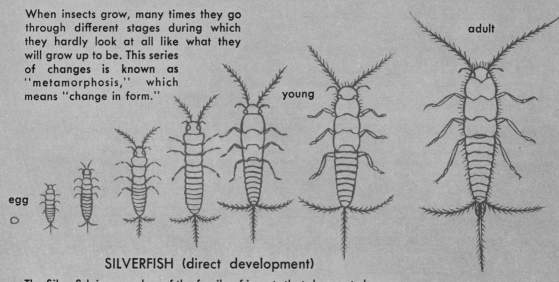

adult

young

egg

SILVERFISH (direct development)

The Silverfish is a member of the family of insects that does not change very much from the time it hatches out of the egg, until it becomes a full-grown adult. This development is known as direct and there is no "metamorphosis."

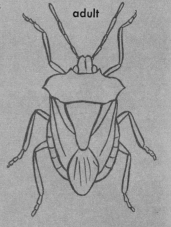

adult

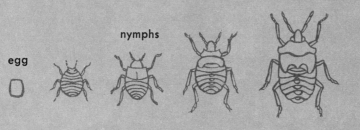

nymphs

egg

BUG (simple development)

Another form of growth is that which is shown above and is known as "simple development" (incomplete metamorphosis). The bug, when it hatches is not entirely different than its parents. At first it doesn't have wings, but these grow slowly as the bug grows. The young of insects which develop this way are called "nymphs," and they must shed their skins several times before they will become adults.

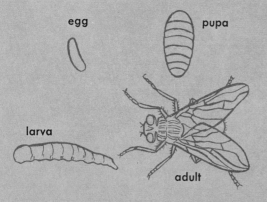

egg

pupa

larva

adult

FLY (complex development)

The most advanced type of growth is shown using the fly as an example. This is called "complete metamorphosis" and consists of four stages. (1) the egg; (2) the larva, which hatches from the egg and gradually grows larger, shedding its skin as it grows; the larva of the moth and butterfly is the familiar caterpillar; (3) the pupa, in which the wonderful change takes place and the larva becomes the adult insect, which resembles neither the pupa nor the larva. Another form of pupa is the cocoon. The pupa of the butterfly is called a chrysalis.